THE MAKING OF

IRONWEED

PHOTOGRAPHS BY
CLAUDIO EDINGER

PENGUIN BOOKS

Published by the Penguin Group
Viking Penguin Inc., 40 West 23rd Street, New York, New York 10010, U.S.A.
Penguin Books Ltd, 27 Wrights Lane, London W8 5TZ, England
Penguin Books Australia Ltd, Ringwood, Victoria, Australia
Penguin Books Canada Ltd, 2801 John Street, Markham, Ontario, Canada L3R 1B4
Penguin Books (N.Z.) Ltd, 182-190 Wairau Road, Auckland 10, New Zealand

Penguin Books Ltd, Registered Offices: Harmondsworth, Middlesex, England

First published in Penguin Books 1988
Published simultaneously in Canada

Mr. Kennedy's introduction first appeared in *American Film* as "(Re)creating Ironweed."

LIBRARY OF CONGRESS CATALOGING IN PUBLICATION DATA
The Making of Ironweed / photographs by Claudio Edinger ; introduction
by William Kennedy ; afterword by Lauren Tarshis.
p.   cm.
The filming of William Kennedy's novel, Ironweed.
ISBN 0–14–01.1191–3
1. Ironweed (Motion picture)   I. Edinger, Claudio.   II. Tarshis,
Lauren.   III. Kennedy, William, 1928–   Ironweed.
PN1997.I63M35 1988
791.43′72–dc19   87–31854

Printed in the United States of America by R. R. Donnelley & Sons Company, Willard, Ohio
Set in Perpetua and Memphis
Designed by Amy Hill and Francesca Belanger

FOR Nancy & Ed
The world's best
Hosts

Fondly,
5.10.88

PENGUIN BOOKS

THE MAKING OF IRONWEED

Claudio Edinger is the author of *Chelsea Hotel* and *Venice Beach*, both of which received the Leica Medal of Excellence. Mr. Edinger has exhibited his photographs at the International Center of Photography in New York and at other major cultural institutions worldwide. His work has been published in *Time*, *Newsweek*, *Life*, *Fortune*, *Vanity Fair*, *Manhattan Inc.*, *Connoisseur*, *American Photographer*, and other publications. He teaches photojournalism at The New School for Social Research and is a staff photographer for Gamma-Liaison news agency. Originally from Brazil, Mr. Edinger currently lives in New York City.

INTRODUCTION BY
WILLIAM KENNEDY

PENGUIN BOOKS

TO D. ANITA

I wish to thank Hector Babenco and Keith Barish for making this book possible. I am thankful to my wife Pamela Duffy for her patient support and advice. For their friendship and counsel I would like to thank Nessia Pope, Mary Ellen Mark, Catherine Chermayeff, Jay Colton, Jennifer B. Coley, Anne Murray. I am especially grateful to the crew and cast of *Ironweed* and to David Schlink of E. Leitz Inc., Robert Olden from Olden Cameras, Harry Amdur and Phil Vance from Modernage Lab, Mordechai Cyngiel of Tekno-Balcar and Ernst Wildi from Victor Hasselblad, Inc., for their constant support of my work.

I thank Gerry Howard, Bruce Shostak, Amy Hill, Laura Ross, Roni Axelrod and Francesca Belanger, from Viking Penguin, for the invaluable input and assistance in the making of the Making. And finally my thanks to Jody Cukier, Vicky Pender, and Paul Alberghetti from Taft/Barish and to Louis Garcia from Tri-Star.

THE CAST

FRANCIS PHELAN . . . . JACK NICHOLSON
HELEN . . . . MERYL STREEP

Annie Phelan	Carroll Baker	Foxy Phil Tooker . . .	Martin Patterson
Billy	Michael O'Keefe	Aldo Campione	Terry O'Reilly
Peg	Diane Venora	Strike Leader	Michael O'Gorman
Oscar Reo	Fred Gwynne	Young Francis . . .	Frank Whaley
Katrina	Margaret Whitton	Youth at Strike	Jordan Valdina
Rudy	Tom Waits	Piano Man	Louis St. Louis
Pee Wee	Jake Dengel	Goblins	John Wright
Harold Allen	Nathan Lane		Robin Wood-Chappelle
Reverend Chester . . .	James Gammon		Nicole Weden
Rowdy Dick	Will Zahrn		Peter Pryor
Nora	Laura Esterman		Duane Scholz
Jack	Joe Grifasi		Matt McGrath
Rosskam	Hy Anzell	Mrs. Dillon	Lois Barden Stilley
Librarian	Bethel Leslie	Young Girl	Cori Irwin
Donovan	Richard Hamilton	Mother	Pamela Payton-Wright
Clara	Black-eyed Susan	Clerk	Boris McGiver
Flower Girl	Louise Phillips	Old Woman	Phyllis Gottung
Elderly Woman . . .	Marjorie Slocum	Bald Man	James Yoham
Slatternly Woman . . .	Lena Spencer	Danny	Ean Egas
Fat Woman with Turkey	Lola Pashalinski	Andy	Nebraska Brace
Bus Driver	Paul A. DiCocco, Jr.	Michigan Mac . . .	Jeff Morris
Sandra	Priscilla Smith	Moose	William Duell
Finny	James Dukas	Raiders	George Rafferty
Guard Captain . . .	Jared Swartout		Robert Manion
Pocono Pete	Ted Levine	Nurse	Pat Devane

Jack Nicholson as Francis Phelan

INTRODUCTION

It is raining on Finny's car, a shell of a boxy old Hudson sedan that rests wheellessly on blocks in a vacant lot on Colonie Street in Albany, just west of the railroad viaduct over Broadway. Two men, fat and filthy Finny, and tall and filthy Michigan Mac, are asleep in the car. Finny is alone in the back seat as Helen and Francis arrive, their breath visible at this witching hour of Halloween, 1938. Francis opens the curtain that serves as the car's window.

"Hey, bum, you got a visitor," he says.

"Who the hell are you?" Finny asks as he wakes up.

"It's Francis. Move over and let Helen in. I'll get you a jug for this, old buddy."

Finny smiles through his rotten teeth.

"Yeah, sure," he says, and Helen reluctantly climbs in and sits beside him.

"Don't be scared," Francis tells her.

"It's not that," says Helen.

"She knows," Finny says with a leer that gives new meaning to the word pervert. "She's been here before."

Francis and Helen say their farewells as Helen settles in for the night, her last refuge from the soul-chilling weather, and Francis walks up Colonie Street, heading vaguely toward the home he hasn't entered in twenty-two years.

It's peculiar, this reality. Synchronous. Colonie Street, one block west of the set, is where my maternal grandfather's large family flourished for two generations; and it was in their house that as a child I began to study their lives. Forty years later, pieces of their reality, much transformed, emerged onto the pages of two of my novels. There never was such a figure as Francis Phelan in our family, which is perhaps one of the reasons I could invent him so freely.

Whatever his origin as a creation, Francis entered the imagination of film director Hector Babenco, and so now, on this simulated Halloween in the spring of 1987, Francis Phelan is fully fleshed in the person of Jack Nicholson; and his paramour, Helen Archer, is incarnate in Meryl Streep. These two illustrious actors, with supporting actors of fine verve and talent, James Dukas and Jeff Morris, plus Babenco, in yellow slicker and railroad conductor's cap on backward, are all reconstituting imaginary history on a street where it truly might have come to be.

How this began, Babenco recently recalled in conversation. He had heard about my writing, and when he saw a copy of *Ironweed* he bought it. Raised in Argentina, later resident in Brazil, Babenco is multilingual, but *Ironweed* was the first book he had ever read from beginning to end in English.

My story made him feel good, and Babenco at first thought that was because it had been his pioneer reading achievement in the English language. "But three, five months later," he said, "the book wasn't leaving my system—the anguish and pain of the characters, the compassion for them. And I decided to move forward."

The novel had been optioned by two producers, Gene Kirkwood and Joe Kanter. Babenco went to see Kirkwood, found that another director was also interested in the book but a year away from actually making a film from it. Kirkwood tried to interest Babenco in another project.

"But I wanted not to be denied," Babenco said. "It was unbearable when I felt so deeply about the material of *Irownweed.*" He went back five or six times to Kirkwood. "It was an emotional decision, not rational. I fought like a desperado."

Then one day Babenco called me, we arranged to meet in New York, and we talked for three hours about *Ironweed* and about literature, on which he had been raised. I knew nothing about his work so he arranged a screening of his fourth and latest film, *Kiss of the Spider Woman,* which was opening in New York two days hence.

I thought it a wonderfully intelligent film, and successfully structured on levels of reality and fantasy, both of which were also elemental to any film that might be made from *Ironweed.* We then went to lunch and in the midst of it I called Kirkwood and said we could make a potentially fine film with Babenco *now,* not a year hence. He agreed, I went back to the table, we shook hands, and that was that. That night the rave reviews for *Kiss of the Spider Woman* came out in the New York papers, and Babenco began to get calls to make other movies.

But he was already booked.

A recurring question asked of me is how does it feel to translate your novel into a film, and how do you do it? Let me begin with an authoritative negative vision of any such effort, this from Ingmar Bergman: ". . . we should avoid making films out of books. The irrational dimension of a literary work, the germ of its existence, is often untranslatable into visual terms—and it, in turn, destroys the special, irrational dimension of the film."

This has been historically true so often that all we can do is hunt and peck for the exceptions. Consider a handful: Vladimir Nobokov's *Lolita,* made by Stanley Kubrick; Steinbeck's *Grapes of Wrath* and Liam O'Flaherty's *The Informer,* both made by John Ford; James Jones's *From Here to Eternity,* made by Fred Zinnemann; Robert Penn Warren's *All the King's Men,* made by Robert Rossen. I believe these are all major achievements in American film art, yet none come anywhere near expressing the fullness or complexity of the novels on which they were based. How could they? An elephant cannot become a horse. But, then again, what does that have to do with breeding horses?

The novel, as receptacle of the entire spectrum of the imagination—visual, linguistic, poetic, spiritual, mystical, historical, etc., etc., etc., until the receptacle is full—can be duplicated only in its own mirror image, not in any other medium. Allow me to use this fragment of a paragraph from *Ironweed:*

> Francis watched this primal pool of his own soulish body squirm into burgeoning matter, saw it change and grow with the speed of light until it was the size of an infant, saw it then yanked roughly out of the maternal cavern by his father, who straightened him, slapped him into being and swiftly molded him into a bestial weed. The body sprouted to wildly matured growth and stood fully clad at last in the very clothes Francis was now wearing. He recognized the toothless mouth, the absent finger joints, the bump on the nose, the mortal slouch of this newborn shade, and he knew then that he would be this decayed self he had been so long in becoming, through all the endless years of his death.

I would like to have that paragraph budgeted for filming.

I'm with Bergman that it *is* rather literarily irrational and doesn't translate into visual irrationality. I don't doubt that some elements of it *could* be translated ("soulish body" would be

*Meryl Streep as
Helen Archer*

difficult), but it would be through special effects, probably cartoonish in their final form and, as such, reductive, with no place in this film.

There *are* irrational elements in our film: ghosts, fantasies, and hallucinatory sights, sounds, and behavior. But these things *do* translate. Babenco and I decided on what would work, what wouldn't. If folks say they don't work, he'll take the rap (so will I, somewhat, and that's all right).

If they say they *do* work we will both bust our buttons.

Film is a director's medium. Yes, yes. East is east. A rose is a rose. Who would doubt it? Well, producers sometimes, writers sometimes, actors sometimes, also critics, charwomen and rachitic, one-eyed shut-ins, who all know how to do it better. But if Babenco isn't in charge then it's the committee system at work, the bureaucratic underworld: Casey, North, and Poindexter, doing a soft-shoe imitation of Ronald Reagan shuffling off to Managua.

Film is Babenco's medium and I sit in the front row of the loge and cheer. I did not *expect* a full translation of the novel. The novel is the novel, and that's still that, no matter what else happens. The fact is, however, that when a writer undertakes the writing of a script from a novel of his own, it is tantamount to self-amputative surgery. You eventually pose in front of the mirror without a left ear, a right thumb, with a thigh partly sliced away, the left leg dangling at the ankle, and then you decide that you're ready for the premiere. Just comb the hair a little to the left, wear gloves, bulky trousers, and a high shoe, and who'll notice? You may even set a new style.

This is not serious. Cutting a novel to pieces is not serious. But shaping a story for another medium *can be* a totally different sort of artistic exercise of the imagination. Consider Bergman's imagination prior to his writing the screenplay for *Fanny and Alexander.* There lay his whole life to be culled for a final, celebratory, five-hour movie. (Three hours and a half in the U.S.) A *fifty*-hour movie would not have been able to tell his story, but he singled out episodes, shaved history here, amputated his psyche there, and he produced a masterpiece for the finale (we still hope he changes his mind) of his career as a filmmaker.

He found harmonies, in the editing of his life and imagined times, that conformed to film size, just as I hope Babenco and I found the same when we structured our movie. That is how it was for me at the start, at any rate: the writer believing he is significant in shaping the film. And he is. But, of course, the process has only just begun. There follows the shoot, and then the editing, and then the screenings.

Tom Waits as Rudy

Listen to Raymond Chandler, noted literary hardboil, speaking on behalf of beleaguered screenwriters:

"If you oppose the routine minds, they are angered by your opposition. If you do not oppose them, they say you are a hack without integrity. What Hollywood seems to want is a writer who is ready to commit suicide in every story conference. What it actually gets is the fellow who screams like a stallion in heat and then cuts his throat with a banana. The scream demonstrates the artistic purity of his soul, and he can eat the banana while somebody is answering a telephone call about some other picture."

Chandler bade a qualified farewell to lovely Hollywood with that essay, and spoke volumes for the eloquent but powerless underdog. But here I arrive in a later year, working not within the studio system but with an independent producer, Keith Barish, of Taft Entertainment Pictures/Keith Barish Productions (and we will get to him), and with a contract that gave as much control to a writer as my lawyer has ever negotiated, or seen.

Would that control have been there if push ever came to shove? I can't say. The issue was never tested. At dinner after a screening I made a remark that included the phrase "commitment to the writer," and another writer-director who was present laughed himself into a clonic spasm.

"Commitment to the writer? In Hollywood? There's no such thing," and he resumed his spasm.

Well, let's put it this way then: This film is the exception that proves the rule. The key has been in Keith Barish's desire to make a serious movie (he also co-produced *Sophie's Choice* from William Styron's novel) from a literary work that the major studios in Hollywood were afraid to touch. Barish, who personally monitored the shooting of the film in Albany, also showed great (and justified) faith in Babenco, letting him run

Carroll Baker as Annie Phelan

Michael O'Keefe as Billy Phelan

Margaret Whitton as Katrina

his own shop with a minimum of interference, and letting him cut his own movie.

During the early months Babenco was approached by several major actors who were interested in playing Francis, but we always had one eye on Jack Nicholson, whose Irishness, toughness, and wit were perfect for the part. No one could remember Nicholson ever evincing the sensitivity or vulnerability essential to Francis's character, but then again had any role ever tested those traits in him?

Babenco visited Nicholson, found he'd read the book and wanted to play Francis. Nicholson then read the script and liked it, and so began the quest to raise the money to pay him his price. I met Nicholson at a saloon in New York one night when negotiations were under way but breaking down. "I don't want a nickel more than the Bank of England will give me on my name," he said with a smile.

But no Hollywood studio was willing to meet that demand for a film like *Ironweed.* And then Marcia Nasatir, who would become a producer of the film, introduced Babenco to Keith Barish. Barish, in partnership with Taft, met Nicholson's price, agreed to finance the film, and became the principal producer.

At some point in these negotiations I was walking with Babenco toward a Chinese restaurant in New York City when the reality of what was taking place reached him.

"We are going to make this *movie!*" he said. Then he clenched his fists, and with both feet leaving the ground, he leaped into the cinematic stratosphere.

He came down to earth in Albany, and why not? Production designer Jeannine Oppewall was sent to check out the terrain in North Carolina as an alternative, but discovered that Albany looks more like Albany than North Carolina does.

And so the movie people moved in and took over Albany's imagination. Celebrity watches were inaugurated to get Jack's and Meryl's autographs. A Hooverville was constructed in the old freight yards behind Watervliet. River Street in Troy was magically reconstituted as Pearl Street in Albany. The trolley came back to Lark Street in Albany, on a block where it had never run. The local newspapers wrote two stories a day about it all, growing angrier by the hour at the absence of openness by the movie people, who were more or less sworn to silence (or else), the press only grudgingly coming to understand that you don't talk about the movie until you are sure there is a movie to talk about.

Some 1,500 locals signed up as extras, and in time some of them would form into a social group and call themselves Weedies. The scriptwriter and his wife, Dana, would spend three days as extras, playing a pair of swells in The Gilded Cage scene, where Meryl so vividly personifies the lost Helen and her vanished dreams of musical glory. Eighty people—crew, extras, stars—would crowd into the long-abandoned Boulevard Cafeteria, which had been reconstituted as a Gay Nineties saloon.

We were all audience for Meryl's film debut there as a singer. "He's Me Pal" is her tune, which she sang for sixteen rehearsals and takes, the final take being, without doubt, the best, and the one that is used. But from the first rehearsal, she owned all of us—crew, extras, all—who wept, laughed, cheered her performance.

Please excuse this total breakdown of objectivity, which is a response to what seems a widely shared perception that Meryl Streep is the best actress alive. Sixty-four people from the production showed up the next day to see the dailies of her performance. Veteran film people, for whom dailies were usually a closed ritual for a select few hierarchs, found the recurring crowds at these daily showings an unusual phenomenon.

Diane Venora as Peg Quinn

Hy Anzell as Rosskam

Terry O'Reilly as Aldo Campione,
Will Zahrn as Rowdy Dick,
and Nathan Lane as Harold Allen

Jake Dengel as Pee Wee

A picnic atmosphere prevailed, with beer, soda, and popcorn for all, and heavy applause followed the screening of Meryl's song, just as it had on the set.

"She rocked 'em," said Jack.

I remember hearing Robert Duvall say once that people *always* think dailies are great, nobody knocks them; and this was certainly the general rule on this film. The excitement was cumulative as the film ripened, as the austere lushness of Lauro Escrorel's cinematography unfolded, as the principals came to understand the characters they had been inhabiting over the weeks. Tom Waits is wonderfully comic as the mournful Rudy, and Carroll Baker, an age away from her *Baby Doll* persona, not only personifies the virginal Irish wife, she even looks like one of my aunts.

And then there is Jack.

He's on screen maybe eight-five percent of the time, in a role he was born to play. By his own measure, the only character from any of his films who is remotely kin to Francis Phelan is Randle McMurphy in *One Flew Over the Cuckoo's Nest*; but Jack is more complex, more diverse as Francis. Jack used to be a screenwriter, used to be a director, and he seems always to be looking at himself as a set of specimens under glass: varietal strains of a single species. In four takes maybe he'll repeat himself once, but the odds are against it. He willfully shifts nuances to give the director a choice.

Jack isn't exactly what you'd call a family man. A nonfamily man is perhaps closer to how he represents himself, and there is certainly an overriding element of that in the psyche of Francis Phelan also. My objectivity falls by the wayside again as I remember Jack's performance in the kitchen with his wife, twenty-two years after he'd abandoned her; and then on top of this his confrontation in the backyard with the ghosts of his entire life. Here is the range of a great actor made visible, the leap from contrition and self-abasement into a fierce and life-preserving anger at the haunting anxieties that are trying to drive him mad.

Francis hears the music of the ghosts in the yard and he moves toward, not away from, them. "You goddamn spooks," he yells. "You ain't real. You're all dead, and if you ain't you oughta be. I'm the one is livin'. I'm the one puts you on the map. So get your ass gone!"

I couldn't have imagined a better performance. (And I did imagine it.)

I say bravo.

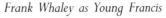

Fred Gwynne as Oscar Reo

Frank Whaley as Young Francis

The film began shooting on February 23, and wrapped June 6, and during the entire time I was at work on the last quarter of a new novel, *Quinn's Book,* which I'd been writing for five years. Ninety-five percent of the *Ironweed* script had been completed before the shooting began, we modified a few scenes as we went, and I spent at least part of almost every day on the set, involved in the production in myriad ways.

But I also worked every day on *Quinn.*

Somewhere in March I made a bet with Babenco that I would finish my novel before he wrapped the movie. If he won, he'd get the box of Cuban cigars I'd been given as a gift. (I no longer smoke.) If I won, he'd owe me a case of elegant beaujolais. (I do drink a glass of wine now and again.)

I lost the bet by six days, Babenco is smoking the cigars, and I am buying my own wine. I do think, however, that this answers another recurring question of me: whether I will stop writing fiction, as have some novelists who worked in Hollywood. My answer is that I am a practicing novelist who once in a while writes a screenplay and tries to keep some semblance of control over what is done to it.

Late in September I went to Los Angeles and watched an early version of the movie on video-

William Kennedy and Hector Babenco

tape, studying it for three days in my hotel room and offering cuts, elisions, restorations, and assorted gratuitous suggestions. I observed, with new incursions of pain, that certain favored scenes were no longer in the film. Alas, alas, Mr. Writer. Once the film is in the editing room your time of influence has passed. Now there remains only that inexorable problem of time, and it will not yield its hegemony over your space.

The full film came to three hours, was quickly slashed to two hours and forty-five minutes, then to two hours and twenty-four, then Babenco said he and editor Anne Goursaud (and with suggestions from Jack) had cut it to two hours fourteen. The editing was ongoing, the shaving proceeding apace. Soon it would be shorter.

I remember a conversation I had with a professor at Yale who said he thought all movies should be reduced to twenty minutes. Was this happening to my story? The worst scenario was Raymond Chandler's vision of the Hollywood producer fifty years ago consoling the writer about cuts: ". . . the scenes that regretfully had to be thrown away were graven on the producer's heart, and in the lonely watches of the night he tells them over to himself and weeps . . . How sadly will he drain the life blood from your story and hand you back the embalmed remains as if it was just what you wanted—or at least what you ought to want, if you are a reasonable fellow and willing to face the facts of life."

Was this happening to me? Well, you knew all this going in, sap. Why are you having illusions about the process now? Welcome to L.A. Welcome to the movie business.

I went back to the beginning of the tape and watched the two hours and twenty-four yet again. Keith Barish said the distributors at Tri-Star were crazy about this version. Soon I would see the two fourteen on the big screen. Babenco called to ask whether he should have an ambulance standing by for me.

And then I saw it, and as I watched I realized that all that was left for me to do was root for the home team. What I was seeing was concision in process, a winnowing of (if it succeeded) a work of art.

Film, it seems to me, yearns for coherence. The novel does also, but the novel can tolerate sideshows and excrescences that wouldn't be allowed by most modern filmmakers. Because the novel requires an exercise of the intellect, an intimacy with the reader's mind and reasoning powers, it can meander and ruminate, it can luxuriate in language alone, and gain in depth from these excursions. But because film is an exercise in immediacy, of raw life perceived in the instant that it happens, those meanderings are judged to be irrelevancies that dilute or divert the principal focus of the story. Stay in the center ring and never mind the sideshows, is the revered wisdom.

I watched the big two fourteen.

And then it was over.

It was better than the two twenty-four.

One of the scenes I'd missed most had been restored. Other things were gone and I missed them somewhat, but not much. The film did cohere. It was faster, better, sharper with ten minutes cut away. Jack thought it was still too long. I didn't. There was talk of showing it to presumably dispassionate people with movie savvy to gain perspective. Babenco was against this. He felt he already had perspective and I agreed with him. To hell with the committee system. He had produced a work of art of a high order.

It wasn't the final cut, it was only the two fourteen.

But it was a work of art of a high order.

That's what I thought.

But don't trust me. I'm only the writer.

William Kennedy
November 1987

THE MAKING OF
IRONWEED

RUDY

He says to me, you're gonna die in six months of cancer. I says, I'm gonna wine myself to death. He says, It don't make any difference if you wined or dined, you're goin'.

FRANCIS

Too bad, grandma. You got a jug?

RUDY

I got a dollar a nurse gave me.

FRANCIS

Jesus, we're in business. But first I gotta get me a goddamn shoelace.

FRANCIS

Oh yeah, the Martians. They landed.

RUDY

Where'd they land?

FRANCIS

Someplace in Jersey.

RUDY

What happened?

FRANCIS

They didn't like it no more'n I did.

RUDY

No joke. I heard people saw them Martians comin' and ran outa town, even jumped outa windows.

FRANCIS

Good. Anybody sees a Martian oughta jump out of two goddamn windows.

RUDY

You don't take things serious. You have a whatayacallit, a frivolous way about you.

FRANCIS

Frivolous, what the hell's that mean? You been readin' again, you crazy kraut?

RUDY

Hey, wasn't you with a woman the other night I saw you? Yeah, you called her Helen.

FRANCIS

Helen. You can't keep track of her.

RUDY

What'd she do, run off with a banker?

FRANCIS

Who knows? She comes, she goes.

RUDY

Yeah, you got a million like her.

FRANCIS

Jesus, God, I'm sorry, boy. . . . It wasn't because I was drunk that I dropped you. . . . All's I had was four beers after work. . . . When you slipped outa that diaper your mother says, 'Sweet Jesus,' . . . and we both crouched down to snatch you up . . . but we stopped because of the looks of you. . . . Your brother Billy come in then. . . . 'Why is Gerald crooked?' he says. . . .

FRANCIS

Where you been hidin'?

HELEN

A fat lot you care where anybody is or isn't. I could be dead in the street three times over and you wouldn't know a thing about it.

FRANCIS

How the hell could I when you walk off like a crazy woman, yellin' and stompin'?

HELEN

Who wouldn't be crazy around you, spending every penny we get. And drinking whiskey. God, you're bad enough on wine, but on whiskey you're a devil.

FRANCIS

I got six bucks.

FRANCIS

She dead?

RUDY

Hey Sandra, it's me, Rudy. You dead or just drunk?

SANDRA

Dnnn.

RUDY

She's just drunk. She can't hold it no more. She's an Eskimo.

FRANCIS

She'll freeze there and the dogs'll come along and eat her ass off. She a bum or just a heavy drunk?

JACK

I always thought you were an intelligent man, Franny, but you can't be, the way you drink. You could be a charmin' man. You could have twenty dollars in your pocket at all times.

FRANCIS

If I had twenty, I'd spend it on her. Don't want her to sleep in the weeds no more.

HELEN

The weeds. I've never gone that far
down.

FRANCIS

It ain't far to go. She slept in Finny's car
night before last.

HELEN

That's the last time. If it comes to that
again I'll get in touch with my people. My
people are very high class.

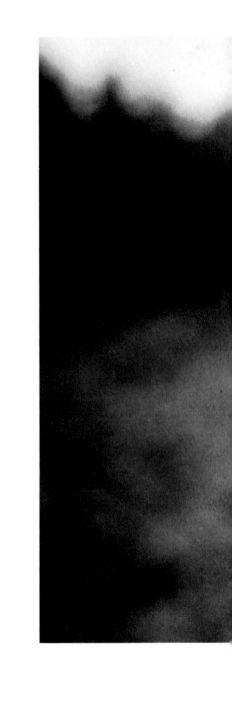

FRANCIS

Who's the guy that didn't make it?

ROWDY DICK

Some guinea horse thief.

FOXY PHIL

What're they chasin' you for, buddy?

ROWDY DICK

I didn't shine my shoes this mornin'.

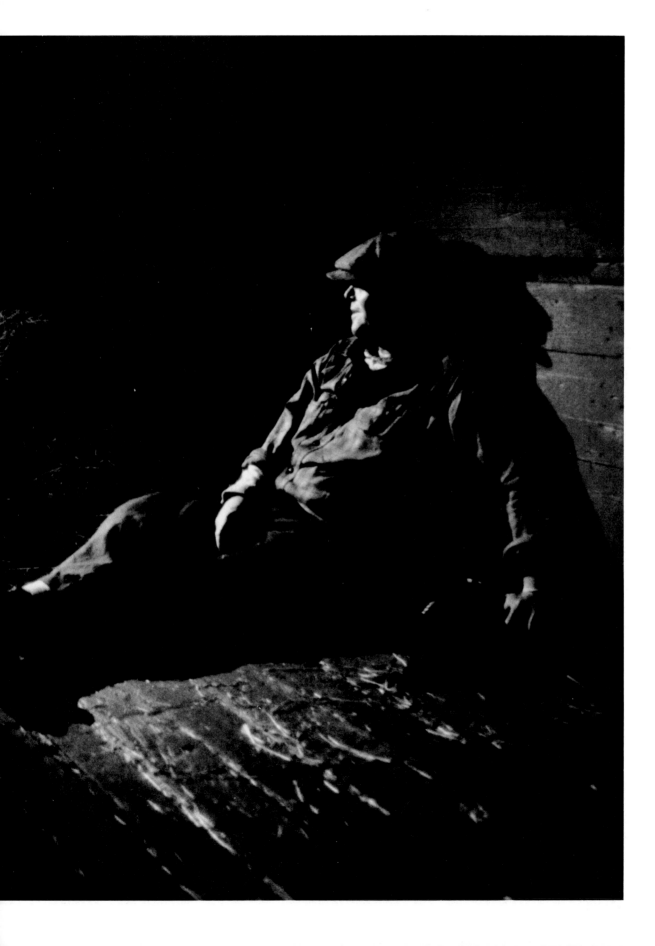

HELEN

I'm not a phony.

FRANCIS

I'm not a phony either.

HELEN

You're not, eh?

FRANCIS

You know what I'll do? I'll knock you right across that goddamn street!

HELEN

You're stupendous and colossal.

FRANCIS

Listen, you squint your eyes at me and I'll knock you over that goddamn automobile. You been a pain in the ass to me for nine years. Jack told me I could stay, but they don't want you because you're a pain in the ass.

FRANCIS

Hey, bum, you got a visitor.

FINNY

Who the hell are you?

FRANCIS

It's Francis. Move over and let Helen in.
I'll get you a jug for this, old buddy.

FINNY

Yeah.

FRANCIS

Don't be scared.

HELEN

It's not that.

FINNY

She knows. She's been here before.

FRANCIS

I'll see you here or up at the mission in
the ayem.

HELEN

Why don't you get in too?

FRANCIS

No, no leg room. Keep the faith, old gal.

FRANCIS
(To himself)

I don't want to die before you do, Helen.
You'll be like a little kid without me.

ROSSKAM

So how do you like it?

FRANCIS

Like what?

ROSSKAM

Sex business. Women stuff.

FRANCIS

I don't think much about it anymore. To tell you the truth, I'm over the hill.

ROSSKAM

A man like you? How old? Sixty-two?

FRANCIS

Not *that* old.

ROSSKAM

Seventy-one here. I go over no hills. Four, five times a night I get it in with the old woman. And you go house to house in the daylight you get offers.

FRANCIS

I never went house to house.

ROSSKAM

Half my life I go house to house and I know how it is. You get offers.

HELEN

Francis is good man, St. Anthony . . .
but how could he put me in Finny's car?
He's so good. . . . He begged on the street
when I was sick and he never even begged
for himself . . . but he put me with Finny.

NORA

I used to hear you on the radio, but then I lost track. What've you been doing?

HELEN

I went on concert tours as a pianist. And I was abroad for years, living in Paris, Vienna, everywhere.

NORA

Oh what an exciting life. I envy you. I really do, Helen. I just never go anywhere. Are you here staying with your brother? He's got such a beautiful place.

HELEN

Yes, I know. It's lovely. We're very close.

FRANCIS

I don't want to go in. I know her.

ROSSKAM

So what's that?

FRANCIS

Mrs. Dillon. I was born on this block. I don't want people I know to see me lookin' like a bum.

ROSSKAM

But you're a bum.

FRANCIS

Me and you know that, but they don't. I'll cart anything next time you stop.

ROSSKAM

Sensitive bum. I got a sensitive bum working for me.

FRANCIS

No ma'am. A spell don't have to be crazy.

KATRINA

To whom have you mentioned my spell?

FRANCIS

No one, ma'am.

KATRINA

No one? May I ask why?

FRANCIS

People with no clothes isn't what you'd call reg'lar business, ma'am.

KATRINA

Please don't call me ma'am. It makes you sound like a servant. Call me Katrina.

FRANCIS

I couldn't, I couldn't get it out.

KATRINA

But it's my name. Say Katrina.

FRANCIS

Katrina.

KATRINA

So there, you've gotten it out. Have you ever dreamt of me?

CLERK

You've chosen our very best piano.

HELEN

Of course. I played all the grand pianos in
this store for years.

DONOVAN

Ain't seen ya much.

HELEN

Francis got a job. It's possible we'll rent an apartment.

DONOVAN

You're back in the chips. Francis comin' in tonight?

HELEN

He might be, and he might not be. It all depends on his work, and how busy he might or might not be.

FRANCIS

Jesus Christ, Annie. I ain't worth a goddamn in the world. I'm so awful sorry, and I know that don't cut nothin'. I knew after I left it'd get worse and worse and no way ever to go back. I don't want nothin' but the look of everybody. Just the way things look out in that yard. There's planty of stuff to say, but it's lousy stuff, Annie, lousy stuff. Yet I never stopped loving you and the kids, and that don't entitle me to nothin'. I went my whole life rememberin' your elbows on the table and that apron all full of stains. Goddamn, Annie. Goddamn. I ain't askin' for nothin' but a cuppa tea. You still use the Irish breakfast tea?

FRANCIS

We had a crooked umpire in Toronto and one night it's dark and we're winnin' but he wouldn't call the game. Old High-pockets Wilson lets go a blazer and the ump calls it a ball. Pudge Howard, our catcher, says, 'If that was a ball I'll eat it.' 'Then get eatin',' says the ump, and Pudge bites the ball, which ain't a ball at all, it's a yellow apple just like this that I give Highpockets to throw.

FRANCIS

You goddamn spooks. You ain't real. You're all dead, and if you ain't you oughta be. I'm the one is livin'. I'm the one puts you on the map. So get your ass gone!

RUDY

Where'd you get them clothes?

FRANCIS

Found 'em up a tree.

RUDY

A tree? You never tell me nothin' that's true.

FRANCIS

Hell, every stinkin' damn thing you can think of is true.

RUDY

Look at you. New clothes. I look like a bum, don't I?

FRANCIS

You are a bum.

ANDY

Okay, Francis. You strike it rich?

FRANCIS

Yeah, here, lubricate your soul. This here's
Rudy the Cootie. He's thinkin' about killin'
himself.

RUDY

I got a cancer. Anybody comin' to my
funeral?

MAC

Probably nothin' wrong with you work
won't cure.

FRANCIS

Yeah, why don't you get a job? Everybody's
out there workin' and here you sit.

FRANCIS

One thing sure, Finny ain't drivin' no more. Somebody burned up his car.

ANDY

Coulda been the cops. Cops was here tonight, shinin' in their lights. Didn't come in.

FRANCIS

Cops everywhere, pickin' on bums.

(Following page)

ANDY

Raiders are comin'. Raiders!

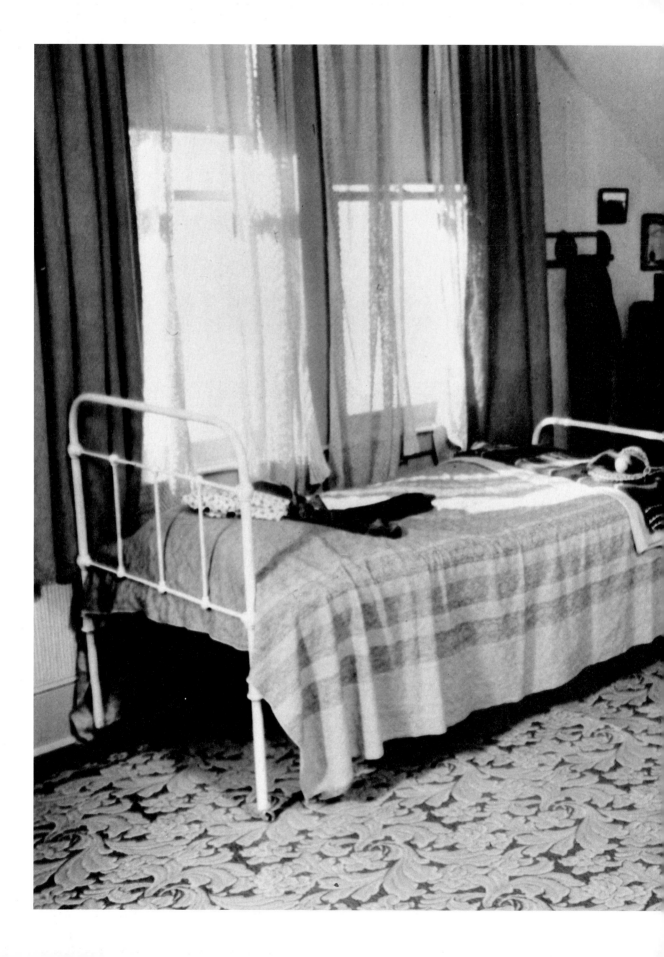

Hector Babenco, Director

AFTERWORD

By Lauren Tarshis

In the hearts and minds of countless Hollywood purists, *Ironweed* is precisely the kind of story that should never be attempted on film. Its story, set in Albany, New York, during the slate-gray years of the Depression, is bleak. Its lead character is a bum: an aging alcoholic who abandoned his family after accidentally killing his infant son. Its ending is ambiguous.

But to Brazilian director Hector Babenco, *Ironweed*'s somber trappings made its broader themes all the more brilliant. And it seemed a natural next step in a directorial career that includes the Academy Award–winning *Kiss of the Spider Woman* but has yet to include a project designed to please Hollywood purists.

"Hector isn't a Hollywood director," said *Irownweed* producer Keith Barish. In fact, the first steps toward the making of the film were taken far from Hollywood: in Albany, where author William Kennedy has spent his life, working as a newspaper reporter, college professor, and novelist; and in Brazil, Babenco's home country, where he first read Kennedy's Pulitzer Prize–winning novel.

"*Ironweed* was the first English-language book that I read properly cover to cover," says Babenco.

"Until that point, all of my attempts to read books in English were frustrated by my poor knowledge of the language. But with *Ironweed,* it was like someone was putting the words directly into my mind."

The book lingered in Babenco's mind, but it wasn't until four or five months later that he realized he wanted to make the film. "The characters stayed with me, like a hangover in my thought system. They kept popping up in my imagination—their strength, their sadness, their need for redemption. I finally decided to contact Bill Kennedy to see what the possibilities were for translating it into a script."

Kennedy was receptive. This was a surprise to some, since as a one-time film critic for the *Times Union* in Albany he had argued that foreign directors shouldn't try to make films about American culture. Babenco, however, was a director Kennedy would particularly admire. The Babenco films that Kennedy saw—*Pixote,* a wrenching depiction of a group of Brazilian street children, and *Kiss of the Spider Woman*—suggested to him that the director could communicate the intensely human themes explored in *Ironweed.*

Within two months of their first conversation,

Marcia Nasatir, Producer

Doc Erickson, Co-producer

Lauro Escorel, Cinematographer
Gus Makris, Camera Operator
Zachary Winestine, Camera Assistant
Pam Katz, Camera Assistant

the two had churned out a treatment for a script. "I think Bill's lifetime as a newspaperman makes him very open to everything that's new," said Babenco.

The task of then transforming the book into a shooting script, which Kennedy took on himself, was formidable. A good deal of the book's power is evoked by decidedly uncinematic elements— the private thoughts of Francis and Helen, the main characters, and in Francis's dealings with spirits of people from his past. While these passages were greatly diminished or transformed for the screen version, the ability of the actors, Jack Nicholson and Meryl Streep, to resurrect and embody these elements *in their performances* is nothing short of a marvel.

The script took over a year to complete. One of the first people then to see it was Jack

Nicholson, who immediately signed on for the role of Francis Phelan. "Jack had already read the book and liked it. I think he thought it was time for him to play something less playful, to do something in which he could really be sour with himself," says Babenco. "He's a very tough actor. He studies and analyzes. He's not a classical actor, who will say, 'I'm playing a bum so I'm going to see what it's like to sleep on the sidewalk for two weeks.'

"Jack was somebody who was reading the book all the time, always going further, trying to understand and absorb the pain of the character instead of just sitting there letting his beard grow."

Nicholson's commitment to the film fulfilled the highest hopes of Babenco and Kennedy, who say they had him in mind when they were developing the script. But it also served to complete the golden triangle—Pulitzer Prize–winning novelist, Academy Award–winning director, world-class actor—needed to attract financial backers.

Babenco's experience on *Kiss of the Spider Woman* had well acquainted him with the labyrinthine process of financing films, particularly those that violate many Hollywood conventions.

Ironweed aroused much more interest than *Kiss of the Spider Woman* did at this stage, but it was by no means a quick sell. "Almost everyone felt it was too sad, that there was no hope," says Babenco. "They wanted Francis to be coming home, they wanted a classical happy ending. I wanted the ambiguous finish, I didn't want to offer remedies."

Babenco found a willing partner in Keith Barish, who eagerly agreed to finance and produce the film. Barish respected *Ironweed*'s somber ending, similar as it was to the ending of one of his past film projects, *Sophie's Choice*. "All the studios had passed on *Sophie's Choice,* saying, 'How could a movie where the two leads commit suicide be commercial?' I guess they forgot about Romeo and Juliet. Anyway, I bought it for Alan Pakula to direct, and it was a big success."

Barish's company, Taft Entertainment Pictures/ Keith Barish Productions, is one of a growing number of small production companies that assume total control for their film projects, from initial financing to post-production. "Three years ago, I watched one of my projects, *9½ Weeks,* get totally botched by the film's financers," says Barish. "After that experience, I decided that if I was going to do the kind of movies I wanted

Denis Blouin, Executive Producer

Bob Guerra, Art Director
Jeannine Oppewall, Production Designer
Berta Segal, Assistant Production Designer

to do, I had to start financing them myself. Now, our company controls all aspects of the movie. We finance it, we pay for production. . . . Having that kind of control produces better movies."

With financing in place, Meryl Streep was cast as Helen, Francis's companion on the streets ("She was the obvious choice for Helen," says Barish) and Barish, Babenco, and the crew joined Kennedy in Albany, where the film was shot.

By all accounts, the atmosphere on the set during the three months of shooting was harmonious. There were problems—the process of dressing Albany in the look of the 1930s was tedious and expensive, and the shooting schedule was hampered by waves of bad weather. But both Babenco and Barish agree that the set had a warm, familial air (Kennedy's own daughters

worked on the set) and a level of collaboration that was, at times, surprising.

"There were some big egos around and there might have been an explosion," says Barish. "But we were fortunate in how well we got along. I'm not about to tell Jack Nicholson and Meryl Streep how to act, or tell Hector Babenco how to direct. And they respect me because of my background and because I was financing this undertaking that many people were afraid to do. And above all, we all shared a common vision of what we thought the movie should be."

The sense of collaboration was furthered by Babenco's own style of directing, which rejects the kind of meticulous planning favored by a director such as Brian De Palma. "I just go in blindly," he says. "I never know what I want

Anne Goursaud, Film Editor

Joe Aulisi, Costume Designer

until I see it all there. And then there's an explosion when everything comes to life. For me, this is the beauty of shooting, the possibility of the unexpected."

On *Ironweed,* Babenco encouraged the active participation of the actors, Kennedy, Barish, and cinematographer Lauro Escorel. "I go in to work knowing that those I'm working with are as strong and as weak as I am. I never see another point of view as a threat to my own creative integrity. I understand and absorb the way of thinking of others."

Babenco took a highly individualistic approach to directing Nicholson and Streep, who came to the set with their own distinct styles of acting. "Meryl arrived with so much preparation," says Babenco. "She knew the insides of her character and all I had to do was shape her a bit. But Jack, he was constantly discussing the material with me. He gets his final delivery on the final cut. He's totally spontaneous. It all made for a very interesting chemistry."

Nicholson and Streep succeeded in bringing Francis and Helen alive with the life force that Kennedy had imbued them with and that moved Babenco to attempt this film in the first place. "I love Francis and Helen," says Babenco. "They're characters who are at the border of death by life's circumstances, who don't have the protection of society or family or money or whatever it is that protects us today. But I think that it's in dealing with death that you really come alive."

■

Keith Barish, Executive Producer